Plants We Use

Lisa Shulman

Contents

Plants	2
Seeds	4
Roots	6
Stems	8
Leaves	10
Flowers	12
Fruit	14

Rigby®

A Harcourt Achieve Imprint

www.Rigby.com
1-800-531-5015

Plants

Did you know that the paper in this book came from plants?

Maybe you ate some plants today.

If you are like most people, your house, your clothes, and your food are made from parts of plants.

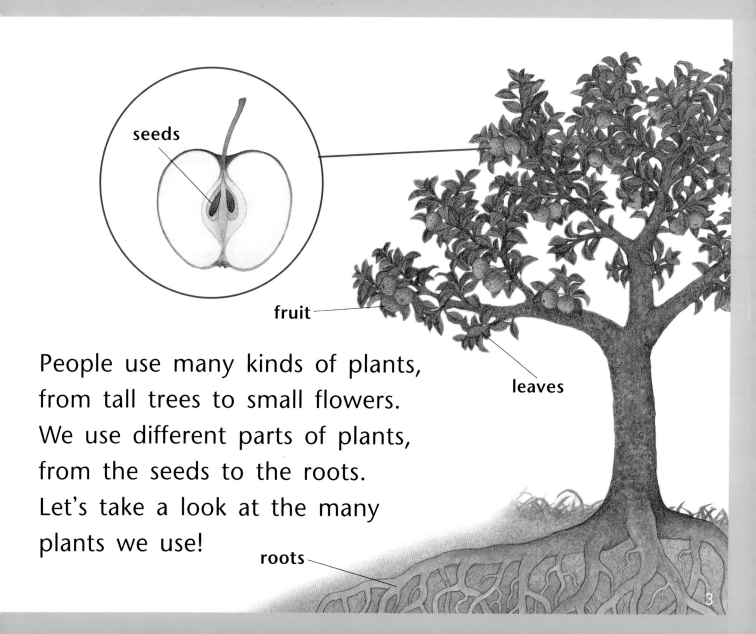

seeds

fruit

leaves

People use many kinds of plants,
from tall trees to small flowers.
We use different parts of plants,
from the seeds to the roots.
Let's take a look at the many
plants we use!

roots

3

Seeds

Seeds grow into new plants.
We use seeds in different ways.
Some seeds like rice, wheat,
and corn are important foods
for people all over the world.
Many other foods and drinks
are made from seeds.

rice

corn

corn tortillas

wheat   **bread**

4

Did you know that some clothes
are made from seeds?
Cotton seeds have soft fluff.
This fluff is used to make cotton.
You may be wearing some cotton
right now!

Roots

The roots of some plants give us food.
Carrots and radishes are two
of the roots that we eat.
Sugar comes from sugar beets,
which are roots.

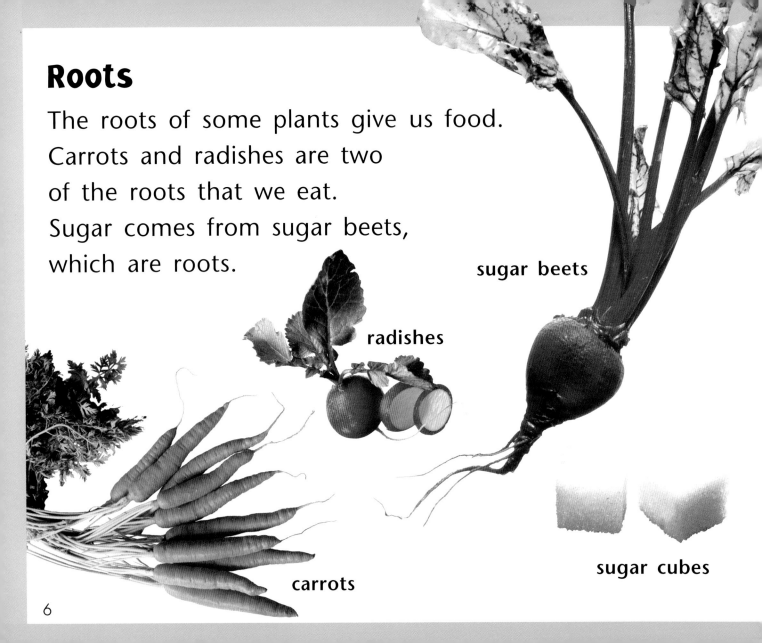

sugar beets

radishes

carrots

sugar cubes

Do you know where root beer comes from?
It's made from the roots of a tree.
Some spices, like ginger and licorice,
are also roots.
We cook with them and
sometimes use them to make tea.

licorice tea

root beer

licorice candy

ginger root

Stems

The stems of trees are called trunks.
People use the wood of tree trunks
to build houses, boats, tables, and chairs.
Paper is also made from tree trunks.

things we
make from trees

We make cloth
from some plant stems
and get food from other
plant stems. Potatoes grow
underground like roots, but
they are really part of the
plant's stem! People from
many parts of the world
like to eat potatoes.

potato plant

potato

Leaves

Rabbits eat leaves and so do you!
If you have eaten
lettuce, spinach, or cabbage,
then you have eaten leaves.

For many years, people have used
the leaves of plants, like mint and parsley,
to make their food taste better.
Most teas are made from plant leaves, too.

mint

parsley

Flowers

Do you like to have flowers in your house?

Most people think flowers are beautiful.

Flowers are used to make soaps smell good.

Some people even wear flowers!

flowers

soap

Do you know that we can eat some flowers, too?
Some vegetables are flowers, like broccoli.

broccoli

Fruit

What kinds of fruit do you like?

Fruit is good to eat because it helps us stay healthy.

Many great drinks are made from fruit.

olive oil

olives

lemon oil

lemon

Some fruits give us oil.

This oil can be used for cooking.

We also use oil to make soaps and to clean things.

We can use many parts
of plants.
We use the seeds, roots,
stems, leaves, flowers,
and fruit.
Then seeds give us
new plants to use!